D0459729

Many Ways

How families practice
their beliefs and religions

By Shelley Rotner
and Sheila M. Kelly, Ed. D.

Photographs by Shelley Rotner

MILLBROOK PRESS

MINNEAPOLIS

DEDICATION

In memory of Margaret Cameron Hood, my Scots grandmother who taught me,
"There are mony, mony roads and none can tell you that one is better than another."
— S. M. K.

For Emily, may you find your way.
— S. R.

And to Hans Teensma for designing this book with
great understanding and creativity.
— S. M. K. AND S.R.

Millbrook Press
A division of Lerner Publishing Group
241 First Avenue North
Minneapolis, Minnesota 55401 U.S.A.

Website address: www.lernerbooks.com

Library of Congress Cataloging-in-Publication Data

Rotner, Shelley.
    Many ways : how families practice their beliefs and religions / Shelley Rotner and Sheila
    Kelly ; photographs by Shelley Rotner.
        p.   cm.
    Summary: Photographs show the differences and similarities between various religions.
    Includes bibliographical references.
    ISBN-13: 978–0–7613–2873–5
    ISBN-10: 0–7613–2873–4
    1. Religions—Pictorial works—Juvenile literature. [1. Religions.] I. Kelly, Sheila M.
    II. Title.
    BL92.R68 2006
    200—dc22   2003019045

Manufactured in the United States of America
1 2 3 4 5 6 – DP – 11 10 09 08 07 06

In the year 2000, the press reported that the World Conference on Religions and Peace was attended by representatives of fifteen different faiths and more than one hundred faith groups. This book is a modest attempt to help young children become aware of the diversity in spiritual traditions and of similarities between their families and those whose faith-based traditions and practices differ from their own. We recognize that many traditions are not represented here and that there may be several branches within a tradition that we have not been able to include.

Parents and teachers will find descriptive notes about the photographs on pages 30–31.

We are very grateful to the many children and adults who welcomed us into their homes and places of worship and eagerly taught us about their beliefs. Thank you.

— S. R. AND S. M. K.

Children go to school together,
work together,
and play together.

And their families enjoy many of the same activities.

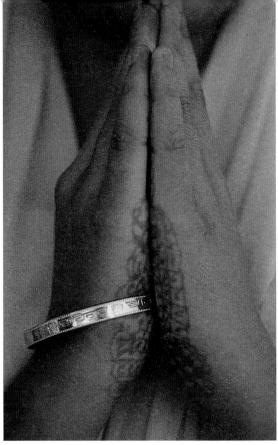

But families may have different beliefs about God.

They pray and worship in their own manner.

Their different ways have different names,
such as Buddhism, Christianity, Islam, Judaism,
Hinduism, Sikhism.

They have different places to pray or worship
like churches, temples, mosques, or shrines.

There, they practice their beliefs and learn

the stories and sayings of their great teachers.

Books tell what their great teachers taught.

Symbols remind people of their beliefs.

Sometimes, music calls people to prayer.

Sometimes, music expresses joy
and thankfulness.

All have special holidays with special food.

All families enjoy their own ways of celebrating
and practicing their beliefs.

All enjoy the beauty of this world

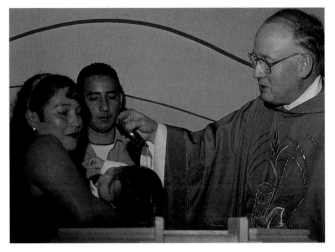

and celebrate the important times of life.

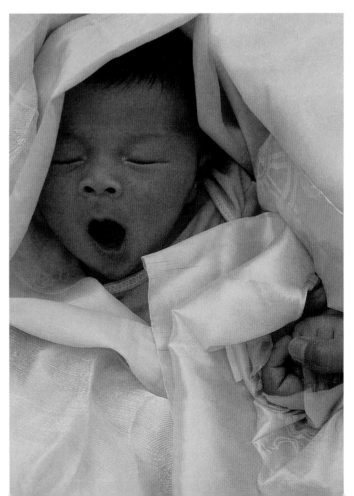

All their great teachers have taught the same lesson:
Love and care for one another

and for our beautiful earth.

Information about the photographs

(Clockwise on each page, from left to right)

Page 8
• A Buddhist child at prayer before a shrine in his home
• A Sikh child at prayer, wearing a traditional bracelet on her symbolically painted arm
• An Muslim child in traditional dress at prayer on his prayer rug (People who practice Islam are known as Muslims.)

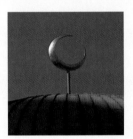

Page 9
• A Hindu child praying before a shrine in her home
• A Christian child praying at her bedside
• A Jewish child lighting Sabbath candles

Page 10
• A Christian family walking out of their church
• A Jewish man walking outside his temple
• The entry to a Hindu Temple

• A Muslim family in one of their prayer positions

Page 11
• A Sikh child worshipping at a shrine
• A group of Buddhists in front of their temple

Page 12
• A ritual candle lighting in a Hindu temple
• A group of Sikhs observing a ritual in their temple
• A rabbi with the sacred scrolls before a Jewish congregation

Page 13
• Buddhists attending a service in their temple
• A Muslim man performing the ritual hand-washing before he enters a mosque
• A Christian minister offering Communion

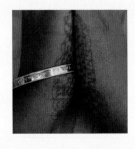

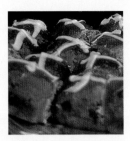

Page 14
• A page from the Koran, the holy book of Islam
• A page from a sacred Buddhist manuscript
• A page from a sacred Hindu manuscript
• The Bible, holy book of the Christians

Page 15
• The Granth, holy book of the Sikhs
• A portion of a Torah scroll, the holy book of Judaism

Page 16
• The Star of David, a symbol of Judaism
• The figure of Shiva, a significant god in Hindu teaching
• A Christian church tower with a symbolic cross

Page 17
- The crescent moon, a significant symbol in Islam
- A Buddha figure used as an inspiration in Buddist practice
- The double edged sword, Sikh symbol of the power of truth

Page 18
- The Shofar, a horn sounded during at the Jewish High Holy Days
- A Muezzin calling Muslims to prayer
- A tingsha, Buddhist instrument sounded during certain services

Page 19
- A silver bell sometimes used during Hindu prayer
- A Sikh instrument used during some services
- A choir at a Christian church

Page 20
- A Christian choir
- A Jewish celebration

Page 21
- A Muslim boy drumming

Page 22
- Food offerings at the Hindu holiday, Divali
- Dessert to celebrate the prophet Muhammad's birthday
- Hot cross buns at the Christian holiday, Easter

Page 23
- A traditional Buddhist celebration
- The Jewish celebration of Passover
- Special food at a Sikh celebration

Page 24
- An Islamic celebration at the end of Ramadan, their special month of fasting and prayer
- A Sikh family celebrating the birthday of their spiritual founder
- A gathering of Buddhist families to celebrate the birthday of their greatest spiritual teacher

Page 25
- A Christian family celebrating the their child's first communion
- Lighting the candles at Hannukah, the Jewish festival of light
- Hindu children at Divali, a holiday celebrating light and wealth

Further Reading

Oneness. Jeffrey Moses. Fawcett Columbine. 1989

What I Believe. Alan Brown and Andrew
   Langley. Millbrook Press. 1999

The Kingfisher Book of Religions. Trevor Barnes.
   Kingfisher. 1999

The Story of Religion. Betsy and Giulio Maestro.
   Clarion. 1996.